Electricity
Makes Things Work

By Linda Bruce

Contents

Introduction

Electricity is a kind of energy
that we use to make things work.

Today, we know many ways
to make electricity.

We use electricity almost everywhere.

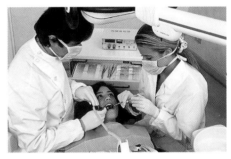

DID YOU KNOW?

Farmers use electric milking machines to milk many cows at once.

Making electricity

Most of the electricity that we use
comes from power stations.
Power stations are buildings
with special machines
that make electricity for us.

Some power stations use steam
to work the machines that make electricity.

Others use water to work the machines.

DID YOU KNOW?

The water flows very quickly
down long pipes
to the power station.

Power stations can make
a lot of electricity.

These windmills are making electricity.
This is a wind farm.
It is a kind of power station.

People build wind farms
in windy places.

Moving electricity around

Electricity flows along wires.
It comes from power stations
and goes to places where it is needed.

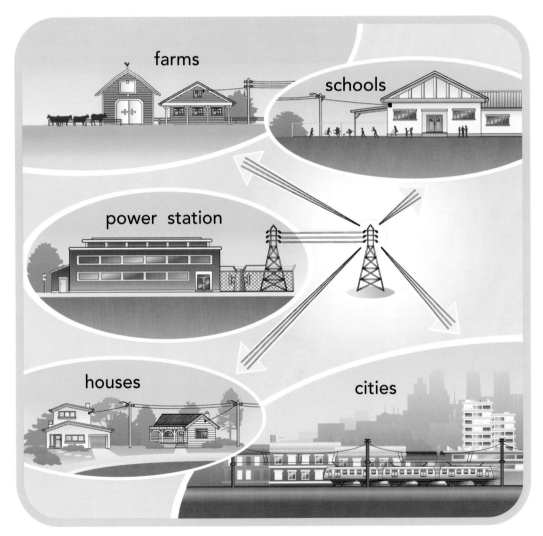

farms

schools

power station

houses

cities

Electricity flows along the wires,
like water flows in pipes.

We cannot see the electricity,
but it is there in the wires.

In some places,
electricity flows along wires
that are above the ground.

Sometimes, the wires are inside pipes
that are under the ground.
These new streets have underground wires.

There are smaller wires inside
the walls of buildings.
These wires carry the electricity
to light switches and power points.

Warning!
Electricity is very dangerous.
Be careful near electrical wires.

Electricity helping people

People have known about electricity for many years.

1799 The electric battery was invented.

1879 The electric light bulb was invented.

1881 The first power station was built.

1920 Many houses had electric lights and radios.

1980 Computers were used in some houses, schools and offices.

2000 Computers are used everywhere: even in space!

Batteries make electricity

Sometimes we use batteries to make electricity. Most batteries are small enough for us to lift and carry.

Batteries are very useful because they can make electricity in many different kinds of places.

We use batteries in torches.

We use a battery
to start the engine of a car.

We use batteries
in some radios and toys.

Batteries do not make enough electricity
to light up homes and offices.
That is why we have power stations
to make a lot of electricity.

How a circuit works

We can look at the inside of a torch to see how a circuit works.

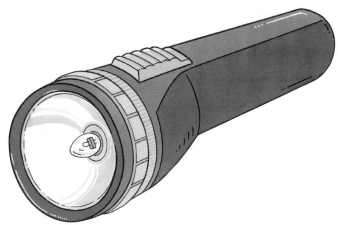

The switch is on.

There is no gap in the circuit.

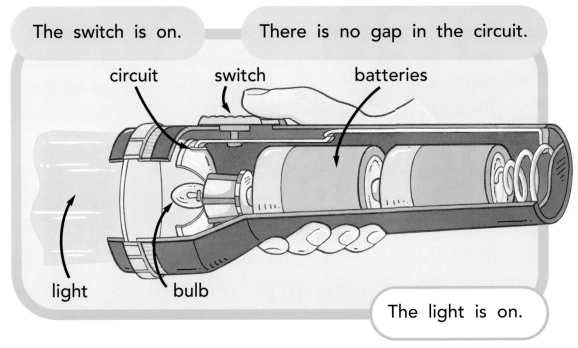

circuit   switch   batteries

light   bulb

The light is on.

The torch will not work
when there is a gap in the circuit.

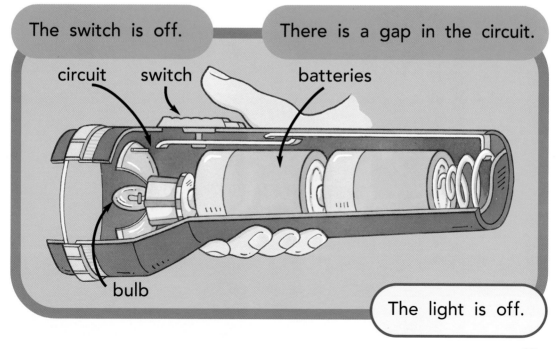

The switch is off.

There is a gap in the circuit.

circuit   switch   batteries

bulb

The light is off.

Electricity in houses

We use electricity to do many things in our houses.

We use electricity
to make food hot or cold.

We use electricity to help us clean.

We also use electricity to make light, sound and pictures.

Electricity in cities

Cities and towns use a lot of electricity. It is used to heat buildings in winter, and to cool them in summer.

Buildings have lifts, which carry people from one floor to another. Lifts need electricity to make them work.

There are many electric trains and buses that take people around cities.

Electric lights make it easy for us
to see our way around the city at night.

Our world would be very different
without electricity!

Questions

1. What do farmers use
   to milk many cows at once?
2. How does the water
   get to the power station?
3. What is used to start the engine of a car?
4. What is a circuit like?

Glossary

gap	a break in something
power	energy made from electricity
power point	place for plugging in something that uses electricity
switch	something that turns electricity on and off
wire	long, thin piece of metal that electricity can flow along